PROCESS OF CHANGE
IN SOLID WASTE MANAGEMENT

PROCESS OF CHANGE
IN SOLID WASTE MANAGEMENT

— Briefing Note —

Mansoor Ali and Andrew Cotton

in association with
Attaullah Khan, Farhan Anwar,
Noor Mohammed Kazi and Jenny Appleton

Water, Engineering and Development Centre
Loughborough University
2000

WEDC

Water, Engineering and Development Centre,
Loughborough University,
Leicestershire, LE11 3TU, UK

This publication is also available online at:
http://wedec.ac.uk/poc/contents.htm

Ali, S.M. and Cotton, A.P. (200)
Process of Change in Solid Waste Management: Briefing Note
WEDC, Loughborough University, UK.

ISBN Paperback 0 90655 69 5

This document is an output from a project funded by the UK Department for
International Development (DFID)
for the benefit of low-income countries.
The views expressed are not necessarily those of DIFID.

This edition reprinted and distributed by Practical Action Publishing.
Since 1974, Practical Action Publishing has published and disseminated books
and information in support of international development work throughout the
world. Practical Action Publishing trades only in support of its parent charity
objectives and any profits are covenanted back to Practical Action
(Charity Reg. No. 247257, Group VAT Registration No. 880 9924 76).

Designed at WEDEC

Contents

Abbreviations   vii

Section 1. Introduction   **1**
    What this briefing note will tell you?   2
    Issues   3

Section 2. Key findings   **4**
    Who initiates the changes and why?   4
    Who implements and sustains the changes?   5
    Who finances the changes?   5
    What are the impacts of the change?   6

Section 3. Cases   **9**

Dhaka, Bangladesh   **9**

Case 1. Night collection of solid waste   *12*
Before 1998 solid waste in Dhaka city was collected during the
day time. A decision was made and implemented to collect the
waste during the night.

Case 2. Introduction of demountable containers   *16*
A change was made to introduce demountable containers with
special vehicles, instead of fixed containers only.

Case 3. Use of Wireless Sets by DCC Staff   *20*
A change was made to provide a wireless system for the staff
involved in solid waste management with an aim to increase the
efficiency of the operations.

Faisalabad, Pakistan   22

Case 4. Clean city campaign   *25*
A special campaign was launched to clear the streets and public
areas of the backlog of solid waste that had been lying unattended
for many years.

Case 5. Cleaning of important roads   *29*
A new team of sanitary workers have been employed to sweep
the main roads day and night.

Case 6. Supply of hand carts and donkey carts   *34*
Hand carts and donkey carts were provided to help with the
inception of a primary collection system i.e. collection of solid
waste from households and its subsequent deposition in the
nearest municipal bin.

Case 7. Waste collection organised by a women's group   *7*
A solid waste collection system has been developed in which a
sanitary worker is hired directly by the local community.   37

Karachi, Pakistan   39

Case 8. Pilot scale privatisation   *41*
The waste management system in Karachi was privatised in two
pilot areas covering 72,000 households.

Case 9. Garbage Train   *45*
The project envisaged the development of a sanitary landfill site
and the establishment of five intermediate garbage collection
points, termed as 'Garbage Transfer Stations' (GTS) within the
city. Waste would be collected from the transfer stations and
taken to the landfill site by train.

End Notes   50

Abbreviations

KAR	Knowledge and Research Programme
DFID	Department for International Development, UK
DCC	Dhaka City Corporation
EIP	Environmental Improvement Project
IDA	International Development Agency
GOB	Government of Bangladesh
FMC	Faisalabad Municipal Corporation
FDA	Faisalabad Development Authority
WASA	Water and Sanitation Agency
FAUP	Faisalabad Area Up-grading Project
MPCO	Multi Purpose Community Based Organisation

Section 1

Introduction

This briefing note is written for organisations and individuals who in one way or another support the development of solid waste systems in low-income countries. It presents the findings of a focused research into the 'actual processes of change in low income countries' carried out as a part of the Knowledge and Research Programme (KAR) of the Department for International Development (DFID), UK. Understanding the actual process of initiation and implementation of change is important before starting to facilitate developments through capacity building projects.

What is capacity building?

Capacity building is the transfer of skills and the creation of an enabling environment to achieve broader objectives in development. It is the process of improving the quality of performance of different stakeholders in the changing state-society relationship. We believe that capacity biulding should start from the existing operational level of individuals and organizations.

Capacity building in this reasearch is about creating an enabling environment for the primary collection of solid waste. This enabling environment can only be created after an understanding of current proctises has been gained.

What is the process of change?

The process of change is the sequence of actions through which the procedures and practices of official agencies have changed with the intention to achieve an improvement.

The aim of this document is to develop an understanding which is useful in making the capacity building initiatives for solid waste management more effective. This briefing note analyses the past changes which have occurred through the input of formal institutions with the responsibility of managing solid waste. It draws lessons from 9 cases documented by our local collaborators in three cities.

All the cases report changes in systems of solid waste management; however, important parallels could be drawn regarding other aspects of urban environmental management in low income countries.

This document is developed around a set of six key questions:

1. Who initiates the change and why?
2. Who implements the change?
3. Who finances the change?
4. Who are the key stakeholders?
5. Who sustains the change?
6. What are the impacts of the change?

After reading the briefing note you will have a better understanding of the on-going development process for solid waste management in low-income countries. This understanding will be useful in the initiation of future capacity building projects.

What this briefing note will tell you?

The purpose of this work is to give a clearer picture of the links between the political processes, citizens attitudes and role of the official agencies in bringing about and sustaining the changes. This work is based on nine cases where changes have been initiated, implemented and in some cases sustained. The cases cover changes made both with and without the input of external funding. We hope that the document will be helpful in extending capacity building initiatives to the local context through identifying the correct target groups and beneficiaries.

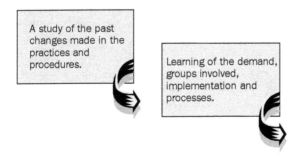

A study of the past changes made in the practices and procedures.

Learning of the demand, groups involved, implementation and processes.

Plan future strategies for capacity building based on the existing practices and past learning.

Issues

- Substantial amounts of money are spent on research and pilot projects for capacity building in low-income countries. Funding is usually from high-income countries and the research findings are disseminated through a number of mechanisms. Local collaborators are involved to promote effective dissemination and up-take of research in order to bring positive changes in the target countries. However, many capacity building exercises could be more effective if we have a clearer understanding of the actual decision making process (called 'actual process of change' in this document) in low-income countries. For example, the knowledge of who initiates the changes and why, who implements the changes, who sustains the changes and how changes are financed.

- A common assumption made in a majority of such pilot projects concern their replication: 'if the project is successful, the target communities will adopt and sustain it for their own benefit'. Further, it is assumed that the project findings will be used in similar projects in other locations. However, past research does not inform us as to whether this actually happens.

- Changes continue to take place because of the pressing need for development. These changes are initiated by different stakeholders for different reasons and may have positive or negative impacts. An understanding of the reasons underlying change could help significantly in targeting capacity building projects to the right group at the right time.

- Capacity building is a part of the social, economic and political environment and cannot be undertaken outside of these contexts. Understanding the operating environment is a prerequisite to understanding who lacks what capacity in any given context.

Section 2

Key Findings

Who initiates the changes and why?

Most of the cases studied have been initiated because of a particular level of demand for improved services. Importantly, demand leads to the identification of the problems rather than the solutions. Leadership at all levels plays an important role in the process of meeting the demands effectively and different levels of leadership are effective within certain boundaries of civil society. Groups of citizens often approach their elected political leaders who are often able to meet the demands by initiating small changes. However, city mayors, administrators and even national politicians play an important role in initiating changes at the city level.

Initiation of change also depends upon who is demanding the solution, as the most powerful groups are usually listened to first. Although powers can be acquired through self organisation and leadership development; poorer, weaker and disorganised groups are generally not consulted.

In only a very few cases is the change initiated because of a policy requirement. This is due to an absence of effective policy and institutions. In Case 8, the overall policy emphasis on privatisation was one of the reasons of change.

> Changes are initiated as a result of a certain demand. Political leadership can meet the demand in return for recognition. Capacity building to take initiatives must be addressed to the appropriate level of leadership, keeping in view both the size of the project and capacity of the recipients.

Who implements and sustains the changes?

This study covers only those changes in which government agencies have a role. However, changes are also brought about by other institutions of civil society for example non-governmental organisations and courts of law. Any change proposed by elected representatives have to go through a set of official procedures before they are approved for implementation. Innovations are possible even in the official institutions provided they fall within certain procedural boundaries. There should exist an opportunity to nurture the innovations from the top management by allowing these to be experimented as conceived. This study reveals that although changes are initiated by different groups, they are sustained by official agencies. Linking changes to local official and political institutions could guarantee their sustainability.

> Government officers need capacity building in implementing and sustaining the changes and not actually initiating them. Municipal scope is narrow and issues which are far beyond the scope of municipal agencies, may not be listened to and adopted, unless they are channelled through the appropriate political leadership.

Who finances the changes?

Local finances can be made available if the change is declared to be a sufficiently high priority by the relevant politician in power. The amounts available may be surprisingly high depending on the priority declared. Changes are also being financed by external agencies which sometimes includes inputs from international experts; innovative changes can be tested in such funded projects, assuming that the donors are ready to accept the risk. Large investments also increase the need for higher cost of operation and maintenance; which is more difficult to acquire. Financing for operation and maintenance is an important indicator of sustained capacity after the completion of the project.

> Capital financing is comparatively easy to fund and monitor as compared to operation and maintenance. Building a capacity to operate and maintain cannot be achieved in a short term pilot project. However, some learning is always there.

5

What are the impacts of the change?
Capacity building in terms of introducing changes is never risk free, and there are always positive and negative impacts. This risk could not be transferred entirely to the local implementing agency. However, it is important to ensure all stakeholders understand the possible risks and to work out risk sharing strategies with the local partners.

Capacity building is about trusting target groups, building confidence among them, appropriately advising them, understanding their organisational constraints and planning some achievable targets.

Important questions to ask, before initiating capacity building projects

1. What changes are intended?
2. What is the method of initiating the change?
3. What is my target group and beneficiaries?
4. How will the target groups and beneficiaries be reached?
5. Is the target group capable of initiating the change?
6. Has the target group introduced some changes in the past?
7. How effective is the target group in reaching beneficiaries?
8. Are there any other target groups not previously considered?
9. What evidence is there that the initiated capacity will be sustained?

A summary table from the 9 cases studied

	Night collection of solid waste	Use of new types of containers	Use of wireless sets for staff	Clean city campaign	Cleaning of important roads	Supply of equipment in a low-income area	Waste collection by a women's group	Pilot scale privatisation	Garbage train
Who demanded the change?	Residents and traders of old and congested city	Citizens overall feeling on the problem	Municipal officers	Citizens representatives	Elected councillors	Residents of the area	Residents of the area	National Policy	Citizens overall feeling on the problem
Who initiated the change?	Elected representative of the area	External donor and municipal corporation	Municipal officers	Country's Prime Minister	The City Mayor	Foreign funded pilot project	Foreign funded pilot project	Municipal administrator	Engineering university students project
Why the change was initiated?	Inconvenience and congestion	Un-aesthetic and un-hygienic conditions	Poor Communication	Un-aesthetic conditions in the city	Un-aesthetic conditions in the city	Un-aesthetic conditions in the area	Un-aesthetic conditions in the area	Better service, low cost and competition	Newspaper publication of the project
Who implemented the change?	Municipal Corporation	Municipal Corporation	Municipal Officers	City Administration and Municipal Corporation	Municipal Corporation and Politicians	The pilot project office	The pilot project office	Municipal officers	Municipal officers and local experts
Who financed the change?	Not applicable	External donor	Government Funding	Mainly by municipal budget	Mainly by municipal budget	Jointly by the pilot project and the users	Jointly by the pilot project and the users	Mainly by municipal budget	Municipal and federal government funding
How was the change sustained?	Through Municipal administration	Through municipal administration	Through municipal administration	The change was not required to be sustained	Through municipal administration & the politcal will	Through users money	Through users money	Through municipal administration	The change was not sustained
What was the impact of change?	Overall positive with some problems too	Overall positive with some problems	Overall positive	Overall positive	Overall positive	The area is clean	The area is clean	Mixed	Overall negative

Section 3

Cases

Dhaka, Bangladesh

The city

Dhaka, the capital of Bangladesh, is a historic city which is nearly 400 years old. In 1830, during the British regime, the then Magistrate and Collectorate of Dhaka, Mr. Walter formed the 'Dhaka Committee' which was responsible for the conservancy services of the town. A budget of Taka 1600[1] per month was allocated for the conservancy purpose at that time. Since then the city has grown in size and population and the nature and importance of the conservancy services in Dhaka have greatly increased. Presently, Dhaka City Corporation (DCC) covers an area of 360 sq. km. and accommodates a population of nearly 6 million with approximately another 1 million daily commuters. In 1991–92, Taka 88.3 million was allocated for solid waste management in Dhaka with a per capita expenditure for the conservancy service of Taka 26 per year. The budget for the conservancy service for the financial year 1995–96 was Taka 180 million which had increased to Taka 950 million for conservancy and lighting together in 1996–97, as new vehicles were purchased. The current budget (1998-99) for conservancy service is Taka 250 million.

The average annual growth rate of Dhaka City's population during the last three decades has been over 7%. Rapid growth of the city has resulted in urban problems in terms of inadequate housing, few employment opportunities and a lack basic urban services such as water supply, sanitation, wastewater disposal and solid waste management. More than 50% of people of the city are poor and 40% live in slums, squatter settlements and on the pavement. It is generally recognized that the city generates an average of 3,500 to 4,500 tons of solid waste per day including the seasonal variation. The major sources of solid waste generation are domestic households, commercial establishments, industries, hospitals, clinics and street sweepings.

According to the Urban Local Body Ordinance of 1977, the DCC is responsible for solid waste management in the city. The main aspects of which are drain cleaning, street sweeping, collection, transportation and final disposal of solid waste. Despite its limited resources, DCC is continuously trying to provide better conservancy services for the citizens. However, due to many constraints DCC now collects only 50% of the solid wastes generated in Dhaka City. The remaining 50% is left unattended either to be dumped in low-lying areas or to be collected by the waste pickers.

DCC has over 5,500 conservancy and 135 supervisory staff for solid waste management in Dhaka city. The cleaners of DCC sweep the roads and clean the drains daily. They accumulate the wastes at the road and drain sides. Once the street sweeping and drain cleaning have been done, the cleaners collect the wastes in baskets and handcarts to dump them in the nearest city corporation's bins. At some places citizens also take their waste to DCC bins. Prior to the implementation of demountable containers, solid waste was collected manually from open spaces and fixed bins and transported to the dumping sites by flatbed, open and covered trucks. Handcarts are used in narrow lanes and by-lanes where access by DCC trucks is not possible. Smaller trucks are used in the old part of the city where the roads and lanes are narrow. Before the introduction of night collection, DCC carried out these activities between 6 a.m. and 6 p.m. The cleaners are allocated roads and drains while the trucks/vehicles have specific areas and routes.

In the last three decades demand for improved waste management has increased because of an increased awareness of the health hazards of poor solid waste management. Most of the groups involved in solid waste management now understand that a good waste handling system is both effective in keeping the environment clean and is financially efficient in the long term. The Bangladesh Environmental Conservation Act 1995 and Rules 1997 also provide major motivations to improve the waste handling functions.

Some changes have been introduced in the system with many groups involved in the process of initiating, implementing, financing and sustaining the changes in Dhaka. These include trained and experienced staff of the DCC, various agencies who have carried out research on the solid waste management system and the citizens. Although all these actors were actively involved in initiating the changes, the demand has essentially come from the citizens and their political representatives. In each case discussions considering the new demands and requirements were held in a series of coordination meetings² of the Ward Commissioners and the DCC officials. Once the majority of the members of the meetings agreed, the decision of any change came into force by the appropriate authority of DCC through general notification to all concerned. In some cases the changes were modified during this process in an attempt to reduce some of their adverse impacts.

The objective of this research is to understand the actual process of the changes and their impacts on solid waste management in Dhaka.

Case 1.   Night collection of solid waste

Before 1998 solid waste in Dhaka city was collected during the day time. A decision was made and implemented to collect the waste during the night.

Who initiated the change and why?

Generally, the citizens felt the necessity for a change towards a cleaner, more efficient, reliable and more convenient system of solid waste management. In particular, the residents of the old part of Dhaka[3] did not like the daytime waste collection system due to the reasons of an unclean and filthy environment, poor visual impact on the city, traffic congestion, vehicular and human accidents, odour problems etc. However, they had no direct voice or leadership to put forward their demands to the authority. Local level social welfare associations, market committees, small trader's associations and representatives from industries and commercial establishments went to the local Ward Commissioners[4] to request night collection. Some ward commissioners from old Dhaka raised the issue of night collection in coordination meetings with the DCC officials. The idea of night collection was also proposed to the Mayor. The idea was discussed in several coordination meetings before the collection time was actually changed from day to night. Most of the ward commissioners from the old part of Dhaka welcomed the idea of night collection. However, some of the ward commissioners from the more recent settlements opposed the decision due to the risks of improper cleaning, difficulty in supervision, and the lack of security of the conservancy staff. Finally, the Mayor agreed to start the night collection service in the city and kept the provision of early morning waste collection services in some new town areas.

Who implemented the change?
The decision was finalised in one of the coordination meetings between the ward commissioners and the DCC and approved by the Mayor. In 1988, the then Mayor Mr. Naziur Rahman introduced the system of night collection of solid waste in Dhaka City. None of the Ward Commissioners raised any further objections. The DCC staff implemented the change through an office order and were expected to carry out the operation without showing any reaction or making any comments.

Were there any immediate reactions to the change?
The working pattern of cleaners[5] was affected, however they were not consulted before the implementation as they are considered to hold a very low and weak position in the hierarchy. They also did not have a professional association such as a trade union or labourers' association through which they could voice their opinions. A considerable number of cleaners work on temporary basis and these workers are always interested to work at any time whether it is day or night. Thus, among waste collectors nobody raised any immediate objection when the order of night collection came into the effect. The reaction of the citizens was gradually expressed through newspapers and public meetings. Some felt that the system was better but many viewed the system as ineffective. However, in general the citizens were not very concerned with the change of waste collection time as long as their surroundings were clean.

Who financed the change?

The change did not require any additional finances because the same manpower and equipment were used and only the time of collection had been changed. Cleaners, drivers and other conservancy staff did not initially demand extra charge for their services at the night. However, the relevant staff are now demanding an extra night service charge and transport facilities to attend their duties as the public transport services are not available at night when they finish their duty.

Who were the key stakeholders?

The primary stakeholders in this change were the citizens and the DCC (including all staff). The Mayor and the Ward Commissioners were also involved and were seen to be acting to improve the solid waste management problems in Dhaka. The waste cleaners were most effected by the change.

How the change was sustained?

Night collection system has several advantages and has improved the overall solid waste management in Dhaka. The change has so far sustained. However, attention must be given to some up-coming issues to continue the system. The demands of cleaners for a night service allowance and conveyance have to be considered with a view to the sustainability of the system.

What was the impact of the change?

The overall impact of the change was seen as positive. The following are some of the positive and negative impacts:

Positive impacts

- **Clean environment:** Night collection has resulted in a marked improve-ment of the physical environment in city areas. It is now possible to begin the day in a clean environment without the unpleasant sight of carrying wastes by open flatbed trucks during the daytime.

- **Odourless environment:** The waste is enclosed at all times in a container and collected sooner after disposal and hence has a shorter time in which to decompose and create odour problems.

- **Less accidents:** The number of vehicular and human accidents in the down-town areas during waste collection and transportation to the landfill site has reduced significantly due to the fact that there is much less traffic at night compared with the daytime.

- **Lower fuel consumption:** Waste can be collected and transported to the landfill site by DCC trucks both faster and more easily due to the reduced traffic at night. This has led to a significant saving of fuel.

- **Increased efficiency:** It has been possible to collect a greater quantity of waste due to the reduced traffic congestion and quieter environment at night. Thus, the night collection has resulted in an increased efficiency of solid waste collection. Regular collection is carried out from more places of the city and it has reduced the possibility of waste remaining un-attended for an extended period, which creates environmental pollution.

- **Increased income:** Cleaners are free during the daytime and can involve themselves in other income generating activities.

Negative impacts

- **Security of female workers:** A considerable number of DCC cleaners are female. In 1998, a few female workers were sexually harassed by some miscreants at work sites at night. This has led to female workers not feeling safe to work at night and want the DCC authority to ensure their safety at work sites at night.

- **Transport problems for conservancy staff:** Cleaners work on a small wage and therefore use cheap public transport services to go to their work places. Such cheap transportation services are not available at night and hence they face travel problems.

- **Security of conservancy staff:** Conservancy staff who supervise the cleaning work are at greater risk from theft and attack by miscreants due to night working.

- **Improper cleaning:** There is insufficient lighting in Dhaka to ensure the effective removal of waste and cleansing of the city. Therefore, cleaning at night is often not of a satisfactory level.

- **More accidents:** The number of accidents on the open roads has increased significantly since the inception of the night collection system. This is due to insufficient street lighting and the higher speed of the trucks.

Case 2. Introduction of demountable containers[6]

A change was made to introduce demountable containers with special vehicles, instead of fixed containers only.

Who initiated the change and why?

Provision of demountable containers and trucks was one of the components of the project entitled "Environmental Improvement Project (EIP)" which was undertaken by DCC in 1989-90 with the assistance of the International Development Agency (IDA) and the Government of Bangladesh (GOB) to improve the city environment. The feasibility study of the EIP explored an

16

environmentally sound, efficient and safe waste management system for Dhaka city. The IDA expert team and their consultants, in fact, envisaged a waste collection system using vehicles and containers around the middle of the 80's, particularly for the old part of Dhaka where the streets are narrow and large vehicles cannot enter. At that time the process of loading and unloading was very slow. The cleaners used baskets to lift the waste from street level onto the trucks. This was not only time consuming but was also an unhygienic method of handling wastes and a health hazard to both operating staff and the general public. The vehicles used were also wasting their time while waste was being loaded. The DCC looked for an alternative system of waste collection.

A further report ('Waste Management Report, Dhaka Metropolitan Development Planning', October, 1992) also indicates that the use of demountable containers was proposed by the DCC officials and their consultants for the old part of the city. This report investigated the feasibility of setting up an environmentally acceptable containerised collection system in the DCC area and compared its efficiency with the system of waste collection that existed at the time in 1992. The reasons for not making the change to the existing system (i.e. collection by flat-bed truck) were discussed with the DCC authority but there was an overwhelming argument for modernisation and significant savings in cash and health over the long term. The report favoured the immediate introduction of a demountable container collection system on a trial basis in the narrow streets of old Dhaka. Other DCC officials who had advanced training and overseas experience in waste management systems also supported the idea of a containerised collection system. This was discussed in a joint meeting of IDA experts, consultants and DCC officials. The idea was welcomed by the DCC authority and the then Mayor Major General Mahmudul Hasan initiated the process of procurement. The provision of this component was kept in the 'Environmental Improvement Project' which started effectively in 1992 due to the long procedure of IDA and GOB.

Who implemented the change?
The demountable containers were introduced by Mayor Mirza Abbas (who succeeded Mayor Maj. Gen. Mahmudul Hasan) in 1996. The procurement of containers and operational details were developed by the DCC staff.

Who financed the change?
As a component of EIP, demountable trucks and containers were procured for the secondary collection of solid waste in Dhaka City. Details of the demountable containers and trucks are shown in Table 1 and Table 2 respectively. The cost of procurement of demountable trucks and containers was met up by IDA funding as a credit through EIP.

Table 1. Details and prices of demountable containers

Sl. No.	Capacity (m³)	Unit price (Taka)	Country of origin	Year of procurement
1.	6	39,204/	Bangladesh	1995
2	12	47,500/	India	1995

Table 2. Details and prices of trucks to be used with the containers

Sl. No.	Capacity (ton)	Quantity (number)	Unit price (million taka)	Country of origin	Year of procurement
1.	3	94	1.59	India	1995
2.	5	10	1.80	India	1995

Who were the key stakeholders?

The primary stakeholders in this change were the citizens and the DCC (including all staff). The citizens saw an improvement in the management of the waste and the DCC staff operated the new system of collection. The DCC staff should have better protection against the health hazards of waste collection as they will have less direct contact with the waste. The Mayor and the Ward Commissioners were also involved and were seen to be acting to improve the solid waste management problems in Dhaka. The IDA and the GOB also had key roles to play in this change.

How the change was sustained?

DCC staff are responsible for the operation and maintenance of demountable containers. However, there are problems of indiscriminate dumping of waste around the containers and some containers need immediate repair.

What was the impact of the change?

Positive impacts

- **Safe collection and disposal:** Collection and disposal of solid waste using demountable containers and trucks avoids the cleaners having direct contact with waste and hence give greater protection from the health hazards of the waste.

- **Fast collection and disposal:** Before the introduction of demountable containers, waste was manually collected from bins placed at different locations of the city and disposed at landfill site. After the introduction of the mechanical means by using demountable container and trucks for collection and disposal of waste, the whole process of waste management became faster.

- **Less odour problem:** Demountable container systems create less odour problems than fixed open bins. Containers are also suitable for carrying to the landfill site without creating additional odour problems as the waste remains covered during transportation.

- **Clean environment:** Since introducing the demountable container and truck system people have taken more care to place their waste actually in the container. Before this intervention, some people used to throw their waste outside the fixed bins which made the area unclean. The new system of waste collection keeps the area clean.

- **Bin in a busy place:** The placing of a fixed bin in any area of Dhaka city is a difficult task because of lack of space. However, as the container is placed temporarily, local people do not seriously object to it. Demountable containers can be placed anywhere even in a busy place.

Negative impacts

- **Access to container**: In some places people dump waste outside the bin due to the fact that access to the container is difficult because of improper design.

- **Reduced capacity:** In some cases, the capacity of the container is much less than a truck. The truck has to make two or more runs to carry the same amount of waste and the process involves extra cost fuel cost.

Case 3.   Use of Wireless Sets by DCC Staff

A change was made to provide a wireless system for the staff involved in solid waste management with an aim to increase the efficiency of the operations.

Who initiated the change and why?

The idea of introducing wireless sets in the waste management system was suggested by some DCC officers and the issue was discussed in a coordination meeting of the DCC. This new approach to waste management created much interest and the Mayor initiated the process of procurement of wireless sets.

Dhaka had a big problem of waste piling up due to the inability of the DCC to dispose it of. One of the reasons behind this was seen as the lack of coordination among different divisions of DCC involved. Uncoordinated responsibilities of various sections lead to delays and inefficiencies. The Conservancy Section of the DCC runs the overall administration and cleaners are supervised by them, while the Mechanical Section (Engineering Section) keeps and maintains the waste collection trucks and other vehicles. The Storage Section is responsible for supply of different conservancy related equipment, appliances and other materials. It is felt that coordinated efforts among all these sections are required to achieve improved services of solid waste management. Wireless sets were introduced in the system with the aim of improving these coordinated efforts.

In the hierarchy of the DCC, cleaners report to the Conservancy Inspectors, who in turn report to the Zonal Conservancy Officers. Zonal Conservancy Officers are again responsible to the Chief Conservancy Officer who is responsible to the Mayor directly. Although this hierarchy seems apparently sound there were many gaps in coordination among the staff and officers of DCC. In this hierarchy, any implementing officer had to physically go to his next higher officer for any decision regarding waste collection problems. For better control, monitoring, supervision and management of the waste collection system, the DCC intended to introduce modern supervisory facilities such as telecommunication and wireless sets like other departments of emergency services in Dhaka.

Who implemented the change?
In 1980, the then Mayor Barrister Abul Hasnat introduced the use of wireless sets in the solid waste management system in Dhaka.

Who financed the change?
The cost of procurement of the wireless sets was Taka 2.1 million. This cost was allocated from GOB funding. The total number of wireless sets currently being used by DCC in solid waste management is 70. These wireless sets are being used by many members of conservancy staff from inspectors to chief officers.

What was the impact of the change?

Positive impacts

- **Quicker collection of solid waste:** Conservancy Inspectors do not now need to go to the Zonal Conservancy Officer for any decision, rather they can contact him straightway using the wireless set.

21

Faisalabad, Pakistan

The city

Faisalabad is the third largest city of Pakistan with an estimated population of 2 million. The city, originally known as Lyallpur had a population of 13,483 in the year 1906. Faisalabad is the largest industrial base of the country, but the population lacks access to some basic infrastructure and services. The provision, operation and maintenance of the infrastructure is provided through two agencies called Faisalabad Municipal Corporation (FMC) and Faisalabad Development Authority (FDA). FMC is an agency created under the local council law (Local Government Ordinance) whereas FDA was created under the Punjab Development of Cities Act, 1976. The basic function of FDA is to develop housing colonies and exercise development control on industrial, commercial and housing developments etc. within its geographical limits. In addition, FDA through its wing called Water and Sanitation Agency (WASA) is responsible for providing drinking water and sanitation (sewerage related) services in the city of Faisalabad. FMC is responsible for municipal services as laid down under its governing law. It is an agency run by the public representatives, when they are in power, otherwise its functions are performed through an administrator appointed by the government. The role of FMC in relation to solid waste management is defined under the provisions of the Local Government Ordinance,1979 as follows:

1. An urban local council shall make adequate arrangements for the removal of solid waste from all public roads and streets, public latrines, urinals, drains and all buildings and lands vested in the urban local council and for the collection and proper disposal of such refuse.

2. The occupiers of all other buildings and lands within the local area of an urban local council shall be responsible for the removal of solid waste from such buildings and land subject to the general control and supervision of the urban local council.

3. An urban local council shall cause public dustbins or other suitable receptacles to be provided at suitable places and proper and convenient situations in streets or other public places and where such dustbins or receptacles are provided, the urban local council may, by public notice, require that all refuse accumulating in any premises or land shall be deposited by the owner or occupier of such premises or land in such dustbins or receptacles.

4. All solid waste removed and collected by the staff of an urban local council or under their control and supervision and all solid waste deposited in the dustbins and other receptacles provided by the urban local council shall be property of the urban local council.

The cleaners are deployed in the councillors wards for the sweeping of streets/roads, cleaning of open drains and removal of solid waste to the waste depots/transfer points which are usually located in the vicinity. For this purpose, they are provided with different equipment such as hand carts, spades, shovels and brooms etc. The responsibility of primary waste collection at a household level rests with the individual households. They are required to keep the solid waste in a basket, plastic bag or similar suitable utensil so that the cleaners can collect from there and dispose at the designated points. Some staff are deployed in public places like parks, main roads, city level meeting places, play grounds etc.

Under the law, the cleaners are required to perform the aforementioned functions during the duty hours for which they are paid by the local council. However, the general practice is that these workers are also engaged in private work like sweeping of houses, removal of solid waste from within the premises of some spacious houses, removal of cattle dung etc. They get additional remuneration for these services, and so try to spend maximum time on these. In addition, they also have to work in the houses of their supervisors and higher officers, who in turn, give protection against any action and/or complaint received against them from any quarter. As a result, the residential localities assigned to them receive less attention. This neglect sometimes causes unrest among the communities and consequently their faith in government institutions is shattered. At times these feelings are vented through print and electronic media in which the very existence of these institutions is challenged and demand is raised openly to close them down.

There are 2503 cleaners on the permanent pay role of FMC. This staff was previously appointed in 87 wards[7] and now, due to the growth of the city, the same number has been distributed in 140 wards to perform the function of solid waste management. Over the last few years it has been felt that the staff strength was insufficient to carry out the waste collection work in all the areas falling within the jurisdiction of FMC. Although efforts had been made from time to time to increase this number all suggestions were turned down on the ground that the financial constraints did not allow such expenditure.

As a result, the environmental conditions in Faisalabad had been deteriorating for many years. The general feeling in the city was that this deteriorating environmental situation was unacceptable and demanded some major action from the city authorities to improve conditions. It was also realised that an improvement in the cleanliness would improve the profile of the city.

The city has not seen many sustainable changes in the solid waste management systems. Some actions have been initiated in the past to improve the cleanliness in the city. Some of those actions are discussed below. This research aims to understand the actual process of changes and their impacts in solid waste management in Faisalabad.

Case 4.   Clean city campaign

A special campaign was launched to clear the streets and public areas of the backlog of solid waste that had been lying unattended for many years.

Who initiated the change and why?

The Prime Minister of Pakistan visited Faisalabad city on March 10, 1997. He met with public representatives and discussed various issues concerning the development of Faisalabad. During briefing sessions, one of the main issues raised was the matter of the unhygienic conditions in the city, heaps of waste along main roads, in the streets, vacant plots and park sites etc. The Prime Minister was seriously concerned about this issue. He therefore issued orders to start a campaign for the removal of all solid waste heaps from the city. He enforced this order by stating that he would revisit the city after a month to check that his orders had been implemented. If there was any flaw or negligence the agency/person(s) found responsible would be dealt with by severe punitive/disciplinary action. This motivated all the actors to perform their tasks efficiently in order to prove their worth in their department.

Who implemented the change?

The local government agencies implemented this change. The Administrator of the Faisalabad Municipal Corporation (FMC) was the key individual in the implementation of this programme. He was assisted by a team involving the Assistant Commissioner and Municipal Magistrates. All the officers were required to attend a daily meeting / review session under the chairmanship of the Deputy Commissioner.

The FMC lacked enough vehicles to carry out this change effectively. The Administrator therefore asked the Deputy Commissioner to form a committee (consisting of the Assistant Commissioner and the FMC) for making arrangements for hiring tractor trolleys from the private sector. The rate would be negotiated to be either the same as or less than the going / market rate. This arrangement was approved by the Commissioner.

This arrangement was finalised and the owners were asked to make available their vehicles at the designated points. The related staff comprising of sanitary workers [5], drivers and supervisors were allotted areas of duty. The points of solid waste removal and the dumping sites were also indicated to make the process efficient. The method of getting petrol from designated filling stations and the authorised signatures were clearly defined.

For the purposes of this campaign, the city was divided into two broadly defined zones namely, North and South. Different teams were formed in accordance with the municipal wards. For each ward sub-committees were formed with municipal supervisors to oversee the day to day progress. This progress was daily reviewed in a meeting chaired by the Deputy Commissioner.

The main issue was to ensure the attendance of around 500 sanitary workers, as well as the operational issues of the workforce spread throughout the city. The smooth functioning of machinery and equipment was imperative, otherwise there was a risk that the target completion date would be missed.

Therefore, additional staff were deployed from other departments and from different sections of FMC to assist the Magistrates. In this way a core team was built to check the attendance of different gangs involved in this campaign. This team reported daily to the Deputy Commissioner about the amount of work done each day along with the plan for the next day. The issues arising on a day to day basis were also reported and discussed in this meeting and the necessary help was sought from the quarters concerned.

The Deputy Commissioner also carried out spot checks throughout the city. This was to ensure that the activities as planned were going smoothly. During these visits he gave suggestions and issued necessary instructions. It provided an additional chance for the workforce at sites to resolve various issues.

Were there any immediate reactions to the change?

The citizens welcomed the change and appreciated this long desired operation at a city scale, which perhaps boosted the image of the prime minister. To make this initiative a success, the cleanliness campaign was widely publicised through print media and loud speakers. The citizens groups were also encouraged to take part in this programme. Hence it was an astounding success throughout the city. Residents took part in the cleanliness of the their respective localities and also informed the concerned agencies of solid waste heaps which had been overlooked.

The reaction to this campaign was very positive. The general view was that if this had not been initiated by the highest level, the state of the city would have remained the same for many more years. Thus the general consensus, as reflected through media, was that the city level agencies should adopt a responsible attitude and run a city wide cleanliness campaign at least once a year. However, many citizens stated that they believed that the government could not do this without help from the local communities.

Who financed the change?

The total cost of this campaign was about Rs. half a million[8] which was paid largely by the FMC. However, a portion of this cost was met by special funds arranged by the administration from local resources by motivating the industrialists and other affluent personalities. An additional workforce of 300 sanitary workers was appointed on a daily basis at the rate of Rs 70 per day. This amount was made available from the regular budget of FMC. The industrialists, traders and businessmen etc. were encouraged to donate uniforms for these workers. The cost of one uniform is around Rs 200.

Additional machinery such as tractors and trolleys along with drivers were arranged from other government departments on which only fuel cost was incurred. In addition, the support of departments such as the Water and Sanitation Agency, Local Government and Highway Department was also sought. For example, WASA carried out the cleaning of the main sewer lines in the city, the Highway Departments helped in completing the patch work of roads etc.

Who were the key stakeholders?

The primary stakeholders of this campaign were the citizens of Faisalabad, as they demanded the programme. The Prime Minister, who initiated the programme has received a great recognition. The District Management was the leading actor in this programme. The Divisional Commissioner was in charge. The Deputy Commissioner was made responsible for carrying this programme forward and to supervise all sorts of activities. The Administrator of the Faisalabad Municipal Corporation (FMC) was the key person to implement this programme. He was assisted by a team involving the Assistant Commissioner and Municipal Magistrate.

How the change was sustained?

The campaign lasted for two months. It took about one week to organise the whole task including details of distinct activities. The Prime Minister due to his other national engagements could not visit the city after one month. However, the progress was reported to him through public representatives and the city administration. The change was a one off activity which occurred because of a strong thrust from the Prime Minister. The lessons learnt from this project need to be incorporated in the day to day running of the city.

Case 5. Cleaning of important roads

A new team of sanitary workers have been employed to sweep the main roads day and night.

Who initiated the change and why?

The newly elected mayor of FMC convened a meeting of councillors as well as health related staff to consider ways and means to improve the city. He stated that improving the condition of solid waste management in the city was his top priority and asked participants to give proposals. Mian Abur Rashid, one of the councillors who has a long history of carrying out different social activities in his constituency, gave the idea of creating a special gang for sweeping the main roads as these roads attracted special attention whenever important people visited the city on official or private business. On such occasions the sanitary workers were drawn from the wards/ localities and assigned to a special duty on the roads on the route concerned. This practice had previously become renowned so that whenever a gang of sanitary workers was seen on the main roads, the general public could safely predict the arrival of some dignitary in the city.

Who implemented the change?

Mian Abdur Rashid agreed to implement this change in the interest of citizens. A prime consideration was to launch this programme with minimal financial input from the FMC, otherwise there were chances of the proposal being turned down straight-away. With these factors in mind, Mian Abdur Rashid developed the following programme of implementation:

· The uniforms shall be arranged on voluntary contribution from different sources such as small traders, industrialists and other philanthropists.
· No additional equipment/machinery shall be purchased; the already available machinery shall be utilized and defects shall be repaired.
· The sanitary workers should be hired on daily basis (Rs.70 per day). There would then be no associated expenditures such as liability of pensions and other fringe benefits.

To supervise this programme a Health Committee chaired by Mian Abdur Rashid with four councilors as members was formed. The duties of the health committee can broadly be summarised as follows:

· To carry out spot checks on the quality of sanitary work.
· To issue instructions to the Chief Sanitary Inspectors.
· To check the attendance of the sanitary workers and supervisors.
· To take punitive action against workers whose performance on site is not satisfactory.
· To arrange equipment/ machinery for the special gang.
· To attend to complaints received from the public.
· To arrange supply of uniform funded by donations from industrialists, traders, philanthropists etc.
· To respond to the suggestions received from any quarter and to attempt to implement them as far possible.
· To raise awareness among road users through mass media (television, radio, newspapers, and general community meetings/forums).

The special gang for sweeping the main roads was created having the following features:

- The gang exclusively works on main roads and is not allowed to be deployed in any other area.
- It has a uniform (yellow colour) for distinction.
- The staff work day and night in shifts of eight hours, and
- The equipment is allocated exclusively for smooth working without any hindrance as these would be available to them all time.

To facilitate the efficient management, FMC has divided the city into two zones namely, north and south zone. Each zone was headed by a Chief Sanitary Inspector and next to him are the supervisors who are directly responsible for looking after the sweeping work on ground. The sanitary workers are required to meet at designated places where their attendance is marked. All the workers are not present every day, therefore, keeping in view the strength of workers present each day, the number of workers to be deployed on different roads is decided on a daily basis. The jurisdiction of each worker is clearly demarcated so that it can be monitored easily and responsibility fixed in case of any shortcoming in the work done.

In this programme, consideration has been given to the fact that there are certain areas which require special attention. These include the commercial centres, central business districts and other important public places. The quantity of solid waste generated in these areas is greater than other areas and is too much to be swept only once a day. It has therefore, been decided that all such areas should be swept twice or thrice within twenty four hours to keep these places clean.

Were there any immediate reactions to the change?
The citizens are happy with this change as the roads now enhance the image of the city. Both the FMC and the chairman of the committee (in a private capacity) have received supporting correspondence from the local communities. There have even been suggestions that the sanitary workers work too hard and should avoid working at noon hours in the summer season (the temperature in Faisalabad is up to 45 degrees centigrade during the months of June to August).

Who financed the change?

The programme was designed to be as low cost a possible due to the possibility of rejection by the municipality. The finances were found within the existing resources available for FMC. The most cost effective option was selected.

Who were the key stakeholders?

The primary stakeholders were the citizens and the FMC staff. The newly elected Mayor and the local council also received great recognition from citizens. On the basis of results achieved so far the programme has proved its worth in the eyes of general public and boosted the image of the authorities who are behind this programme.

How the change was sustained?

The change was introduced in February, 1999. To date the programme is being run very effectively due to constant monitoring by the initiators of change. However, it is hard to predict its future continuation and consistency. It is assumed that the citizens will complain in the event of the discontinuation of this programme. This element of public awareness is crucial for sustaining such programmes. Based on our past experience regarding the working style of government institutions, we can not solely entrust this responsibility to the government functionaries to continue it.

What was the impact of change?

Positive impacts

■ **Less hinderance.** At night hours, the volume of traffic decreases and hence these roads are free from all sorts of hindrance caused during the day times.

■ **Fewer accidents.** The night duty provides an opportunity for easy movement for the sanitary workers combined with safety against accidents/ mishaps.

■ **Increased efficiency.** While working in the hazard free environment at night hours, the efficiency of work has increased greatly compared to daytime work.

- **Easier for morning staff.** Having swept the main roads at night, the volume of work was much reduced in the morning. So the daytime staff were able to perform the sweeping more easily.

- **Better service.** The quantity of solid waste was too much to be handled in full by the staff working during day hours only, resulting in the piling up of solid waste on the road side. With the new arrangement (night duty), it was possible to dispose of the whole quantity of solid waste.

- **Less dust.** People often complained about the spreading of dust in the day time which spoiled their neat clothes. The inhalation of dust was also problematic from a health perspective especially for those suffering from asthma and dust allergies. This problem is now solved as a large quantity of dust is removed at night with little left for daytime.

Case 6. Supply of hand carts and donkey carts in Shadab Colony

Hand carts and donkey carts were provided to help with the inception of a primary collection system i.e. collection of solid waste from households and its subsequent deposition in the nearest municipal bin.

Who initiated the change?

The change was initiated as a result of The Faisalabad Area Upgrading Project (FAUP)[9] funded by the Governments of Pakistan and DFID, UK. Discussions were initiated by the FAUP staff with the residents of Shadab Colony regarding a solid waste system to be operated by the community. It aims to improve the quality of life for the poor communities in the slums and katchi abadies[10] in Faisalabad. FAUP is providing support to strengthen the existing capacity of the community by providing technical assistance and a supply of vehicles.

The activity was initiated in Shadab Colony, which is a slum area of over 100 acres of land and with a population of 20,000. The communities were initially reluctant to run a solid waste system as they thought it was exclusively the responsibility of the government through FMC. They immediately showed concern about the apparent double payment for a service for which they already pay through their taxes. The process of mobilization was continued for months, during which the issue was discussed from different perspectives to try to convince them of the potential benefits of such a system. Examples were quoted where the communities had launched this system and were running it successfully. To assist them further, it was considered appropriate to help one Multipurpose Community Organisations (MPCOs) in each project area, who agreed to run this programme, by providing two hand carts and one donkey cart, free of cost as a demonstration project. The programme was finally initiated as an outcome of discussions with the communities through both male and female MPCOs of the area.

Who implemented the change?

Eight hand carts and four donkey carts were prepared in local workshops. These were handed over to the MPCOs under certain conditions mentioned in the terms of partnership (TOP) signed between FAUP and the MPCO executive members. The equipment was designed by a UK consultant who has enormous international experience in the field. The process of design was started through discussions with the field teams and community members, followed by a visit to the areas to grasp the physical conditions on ground. This provided an opportunity to see the street widths, the location of transfer points and the distance to different transfer points in each locality. The consultant also had meetings with FMC staff including medical officers, health officers, chief sanitary inspectors and other inspectors. He also discussed with sanitary workers, the ultimate users of the equipment, and got their views based on their previous experience. The design of existing carts was also taken into account. This data and information collected through different sources was the basis of developing the appropriate design model of hand and donkey carts. After the design was completed, sample carts were prepared. These were then tested, and related personnel from FMC and FAUP were invited to see the demonstration. The comments of all concerned were considered to try to improve the design.

The field team monitored the process of implementation of this programme. The team worked in close co-ordination with the local communities and motivated one neighbourhood level MPCO to run this programme through community involvement. After initial discussions and dialogues and the incorporation of the community's suggestions, general consent of the members was given regarding their willingness to contribute to this system. Subsequently the search for a suitable sanitary worker who could render the service regularly was started. During this process, it was decided to involve the FMC sanitary worker (who was appointed in this colony recently through MPCO's efforts but his performance was not satisfactory) by asking him to get assistance from his family. This was thought essential for two reasons: one, to cater for the legal aspect according to which a person being an employee of the government can not render his services privately during duty hours and two, to avoid confrontation between the FMC worker and the privately hired worker. Hence, the FMC sanitary worker arranged to involve his wife in this activity and a level of payment was agreed with him. This arrangement was discussed with the community members in a meeting. The members approved the agreement made with the sanitary worker.

Who financed the change?

An initial input was provided by the FAUP who provided assistance in the motivation of the communities and helped in the design of the carts. They also provided the initial eight hand carts and four donkey carts. Once underway, the system was funded by the inhabitants of the area who agreed to contribute Rs 20 per household per month for this system. A donkey for the cart was required to be purchased for which the MPCO gave a loan of Rs.3,000 to the sanitary worker, which he returned in installments.

How the change was sustained?

The system of solid waste was launched in 1997 in one neighbourhood. Since then this system has been running successfully. This is due to the fact that the community members have seen the benefits of this programme. The community members are collecting the contribution on a monthly basis and keeping it in a MPCO joint account. The amount is then paid in lump sum at the end of each month. The experience of involving the FMC sanitary worker has proved quite successful. Being husband and wife, the members coordinate the work which is being carried out smoothly.

What was the impact of change?

Although residents of the area are making a regular financial contribution, the area is clean and the system has overall positive impacts. There was no service in the area before and now there is a waste collection service available.

Case 7. Waste collection organised by a women's group in Chak-7

A solid waste collection system has been developed in which a sanitary worker is hired directly by the local community.

Who initiated the change?

Chak-7 is a low income area comprising of 75 acres of land and having population of 15,000. The issues and options regarding solid waste were discussed in different meetings arranged by FAUP. Residents were not satisfied with the level of the solid waste management service. The members of a womens organization, named CARWAN, took the initiative to improve solid waste disposal by hiring a waste collector for drain cleaning, street sweeping and waste collection. Lane level organizations had already been formed in this neighbourhood in early 1996 but were mostly engaged in poultry keeping. Due to the limitation of lane level activities, they decided to broaden their activities to cover the remaining area also and started working in a more organised way. The women of the three existing organizations and representatives from other lanes agreed to form a neighbourhood level organisation. Consequently, ten members were selected, 2 from each lane. This group conducts regular meetings and discusses the issues on a day to day basis. Every decision needs the approval of members in a general body meeting. Its president and secretary were elected democratically. The name of the organisation was proposed as "CARWAN" which is interpreted by one member as that they will act like a convoy on the road of development. They have representation in an elected body from five lanes. In order to include members from other lanes the president and secretary have planned meetings in the remaining lanes.

Who implemented the change?

CARWAN has implemented the changes by hiring a sanitary worker who is responsible for sweeping the lanes, collection of waste from the houses and collection of silt from drains.

Who financed the change?

The hand cart for collection of waste was provided by FAUP through signing of an agreement with CARWAN. The residents contribute Rs.15 per house per month, to pay for the sanitary worker, purchase necessary equipment and for maintenance. The task of collecting the monthly contribution has been assigned to a representative in each lane. The amount collected is then deposited in the MPCO's joint bank account.

How the change was sustained?

This system is running smoothly and every member is taking an active part. By observing its impact, more lanes from other neighborhoods have shown an interest to start a similar programme. This has led to an increase in the demand for women of other neighborhoods for similar systems, reflecting the change in attitude of the residents towards the solution of this problem.

Karachi, Pakistan

The city

Karachi is the largest city of Pakistan, a home to over 10 million people. The main components of urban solid waste management are faced with a major crisis because of the large size of city and rapid population growth. One of the major concerns from the local pressure groups is a serious lack of long term plans, which result in a number of disjointed, ad-hoc and often counter productive policies, plans and administrative frameworks.

Karachi Metropolitan Corporation (KMC) is the responsible agency for solid waste management. The city administration is divided into five District Municipal Corporations (DMCs), corresponding to the five administrative divisions of Karachi (Districts South, Central, East, West and Malir). The DMCs work almost independently of KMC's control and are fundamentally responsible for solid waste collection. Together they provide services to 80% of the city but are able to collect only an estimated 30—40% of the 6000—8000 tons of solid waste generated daily. The solid waste that is collected is not properly disposed of as it either does not reach the existing final disposal or is disposed at the ultimate disposal sites in a non-engineered and un-safe manner, mostly by open burning.

Sanitary workers are employed by DMCs to sweep streets and are often hired by residents to provide a primary waste collection service. The service is not provided by the city district municipal agencies themselves, but the sweepers, who are entrusted with the job of sweeping the streets, put in extra time to perform the door to door collection service and charge the individual households for the service. Recently some private entrepreneurs, mostly refugees from Afghanistan have entered into the field of waste collection.

From the households, the waste is taken to neighbourhood collection points (concrete and steel bins) stationed at roadsides, on pathways, in parks and playgrounds. In such places, the waste is either burnt or is collected by the municipal agency's waste vans and transported to various disposal sites (non-engineered sites, where waste is dumped and openly burnt) located on the outskirts of the city. However, a large amount of waste is thrown in open spaces, like parks, playgrounds, empty plots, on roadsides, in nullahs etc. Consequently, much of the garbage remains uncollected.

Efforts have been made in the past to increase the waste load carrying capacity of KMC by providing more and more mechanised systems such as trucks, dumpers, loaders etc. These measures have not yielded the required results. Substantial investment has been made by KMC in improving the solid waste management systems of Karachi. A number of changes have been initiated by different stakeholders. Two major changes for the city are discussed below.

Case 8.   Pilot scale privatisation

The waste management system in Karachi was privatised in two pilot areas covering 72,000 households.

Who initiated the change?

The Municipal Corporation of District Central of Karachi took the initiative to privatise the solid waste management services. Although, privatisation of various segments of the system had also been recommended by consultants hired by KMC. The perceived objectives of introducing privatisation were to introduce competition and an improved level of services. In the past few years, the national government and all tiers of governance i.e. federal, provincial and local, has taken to the idea of privatisation. In addition to the privatisation of the industrial and service sectors, (such as banking institutions), the process of privatisation of municipal services have also been promoted. The reasons for this include a control on growing corruption, politicisation and lack of transparency in functions, both administrative and financial. Steady and continuous decline in levels of service and a lack of long term vision. Also, the extremely low salary scales of staff and supporting funds prohibit the introduction of skilled technical staff, needed to boost the efficiency levels of the organisations. It has been argued, that all these factors have led to significant deterioration in service delivery capacity of the civic organisations, leading to continuous system defects, breakdowns and malfunctions. Privatisation has been seen as an option to control some of these problems.

Who implemented the change?

Tenders were floated by DMC Central office and a contract was signed with the lowest bidder, Al-Khalid Agencies for Waste Management on 26 September 1998. The service area included 12 Councillor's Wards in F. B. Area, comprising of 25,000 households and 4 Councillor's Wards in North Karachi comprising of 47,000 households making a total of 72, 000 households. The estimated quantities were 1350 tonnes / day. The total value of the contract was Rs.43,500,000/- and the contract duration was one year, with the provision for further renewal on the successful completion of the first stage.

The tasks identified in the contract included, door to door collection of waste and sweeping in all said zones (residential, commercial, industrial, hospitals, clinics, laboratories, schools, markets, marriage halls, restaurants or any other type of establishment) and sweeping of all roads, streets, footpaths, service roads, central islands, removal of debris, building material waste, dead animals, birds, cleaning of storm water drains, nallahs and removal of offals and related wastes, etc. generated there at.

The waste after collection was to be transported and disposed of on a daily basis to the newly developed landfill site at Deh Jam Chakro (or any other nominated site). Al-Khalid Agencies were authorised to use the existing waste collection facilities at the neighbourhood level and also arrange for new areas as and when required. They were also required to carry out anti-mosquito drives, at least once a month. Al-Khalid were prohibited from burning the waste, both allowing or indulging themselves in scavenging (waste picking) activities and their sanitary staff were bound by the contract to wear distinctive uniforms.

The private contractors were not allowed to employ or hire full or part time services of sanitary workers and any other staff, in the service of DMC Central or any other local body, and they were bound by the contract to both acquire and maintain from their own resources all the required equipment and machinery such as dumpers / loaders, waste vans, etc. The imparting of public education through information leaflets was also part of the contract agreement. Subject to satisfactory performance, payment was to be made on a weekly basis.

Who financed the change?

The total value of the contract was Rs 43,500,000/- for a period of one year. Funds for the project were made available from the existing expense head for similar services previously carried out by the DMC staff themselves and the sanitary staff made redundant as a result of the privatisation were adjusted elsewhere in the system. No lay-offs were made other than those of 'ghost workers' [those who are on pay roll but do not attend duties].

Who were the key stakeholders?

The major stakeholders in this process of change were DMC Central and the private contractors, Al-Khalid Agencies for Waste Management. However, the residents of the area that was to receive this service, can also be identified as key participants of the process, being the direct beneficiaries or otherwise of the project. The sanitary workers already working in the area were also key stakeholders as they may loose their additional income from the primary collection tasks.

How the change was sustained?

A number of lessons were learned after the experience of the first year. Many problems were encountered and the waste management system in the city did not improve as expected. However, after extensive negotiations, in August, 1999, the contract of Al-Khalid has been renewed by DMC Central. The change is so far sustainable and DMC has continued the financing of the project.

What was the impact of change?

Positive impacts

- **A new management concept.** The project has managed to introduce a new concept of solid waste management, which resulted in the capacity building of the private contractor and DMC's staff.

- **Capacity building.** The project has also led to a capacity building in terms of identifying problems and bottlenecks. The fact that the project has survived one year of its operation demonstrates that both parties retain sufficient faith in the sustainability of this process of change.

Negative impacts

- **Lack of public participation.** It was reported that primary collection was still done by DMC waste collectors. Citizens are not concerned about who is collecting waste, as long as they get a service.

- **Discouragement of recycling/resource recovery.** Reference can be made to the Clause 12 of the contract, where the private contractor is prohibited from either allowing or himself taking part in scavenging activities and 100% waste is required to be dumped in the landfill site.

Consequently, no efforts were made on the part of project partners to educate the public in various options of waste management at the household level. It is just a collect – transport – dump project. Wider aspects of the issue have not been considered. So, it seems that a good opportunity for carrying out various useful experiments, which could even have made the project more manageable, people friendly, participatory and cost effective, has been missed.

Case 9.   Garbage Train

The project envisaged the development of a sanitary landfill site and the establishment of five intermediate garbage collection points, termed as 'Garbage Transfer Stations' (GTS) within the city. Waste would be collected from the transfer stations and taken to the landfill site by train.

Who initiated the change?
The concept for this project was first developed in a Final Year Civil Engineering project 'A Feasibility Study of the Railway-Trucking Integrated Network for Solid Waste Management in Karachi', of NED University of Engineering & Technology, Karachi. The project was undertaken in 1992, and was the initiative of Prof. Saeed Ahmed Khan, a professor of environmental

engineering at the NED University, who acted as Project Advisor on this student project. In this report, the basic concept for the transportation and waste management model for the project was developed. The project received good publicity in the local press and the idea was adopted by KMC. In the last quarter of 1994, the project was given the go-ahead by the then Administrator of KMC, Mr. Fahim-uz-Zaman as a part of the then Prime Minister's Development Package for the city. Although a proposal previously existed to develop landfill sites for the city, the option of availing the rail service as a mode of solid waste transportation and its integration with the existing trucking service was never considered or discussed before.

The decision to initiate this project was taken internally within KMC and the project was not open to any kind of public debate nor was the idea discussed with other stakeholders in this sector. It is also interesting to note that most of the project related work, particularly at the decision making level was handled by a small staff of engineers hand picked by the then Administrator and was not routed through the normal KMC official hierarchy. This was apparently done to facilitate the rapid progress of the project, which was considered to be on the high priority list of the Administrator KMC. The department of Solid Waste Management, KMC, managed this project.

Who implemented the change?
The sponsoring, execution, operation and maintenance of the project was to be the responsibility of KMC and the project was expected to be completed in a period of twelve months (starting in the last quarter of 1994). The private sector was invited to handle some specific activities of the project. The contract for the loading of solid waste on to the train wagons at the transfer stations and unloading of the waste at the landfill site was awarded to a private contractor.

The practices for primary collection of solid waste were to remain the same. However, instead of the solid waste being transported to the final disposal site directly, as in the past, it was to be transferred to an intermediate transfer station.

The operations planned to be performed at the transfer station included:

· Dumping of solid waste from vehicles.
· Use of conveyers for movement.

- Compaction of solid waste into 20 feet containers for onward transportation up to railway yard.
- Bulk transportation of compacted solid waste by trains up to landfill site.
- Disposal at landfill site.

It was agreed that Pakistan Railways were to provide 72 specially designed train wagons on a daily basis, which were to be used to transfer the waste from the transfer stations to the Dhabeji landfill site. However, this component of the project soon ran into trouble because of lack of co-ordination between the KMC and Pakistan Railways, a decisive factor in the ultimate closure of the project.

The process of transporting solid waste from the Wazir Mansion Railway Station to Dhabeji Landfill site continued for about three months. On average only about 25—30 wagons were provided by Pakistan Railways, instead of the committed figure of 72. At times even the locomotive engine failed to turn up, thus bringing the entire operation to a halt. Even the wagons that were provided were defective, in an extremely run down condition and totally unsuitable for the required job. The burning of solid waste also continued at various stages. This burning garbage was loaded on to the wagons which resulted in extremely hazardous conditions.

A private contractor, Jammy Constructors (pvt) Ltd. was awarded the contract of loading waste into the wagons at the Wazir Mansion Transfer station and unloading the same at the Dhabeji Station and also transporting it to the actual landfill site. The contractor was to provide all the machinery needed for job. They were to be paid a daily amount of Rs.25,000/- for the loading of up to 72 wagons, and Rs.85,000/- for the unloading and subsequent transportation to the actual landfill site of the waste from the 72 wagons. Certain clauses in the contract like payment on a daily basis and payment even when the train failed to make a trip caused problems for KMC later on as the contractor had to be paid on several occasions for idle hours.

As the proposed sanitary landfill site was at a distance from the main railway line at Dhabeji, the first requirement at one site was the laying out of additional railway tracks from the main railway and the laying out of a link road. This task was given by KMC to Pakistan Railways and an amount of Rs 15 million (from the own funds of KMC) was released to Pakistan Railways for the purpose. This task was almost completed by Pakistan Railways engineers and KMC also constructed an unloading platform at the site.

Who financed the change?

The project was mainly funded by local funds available by KMC. Additional grant was given by the federal government. The cost of various components of the project is known, however, because of the nature of the project, the total cost is not known.

Who were the key stakeholders?

The 'Garbage Train' project dealt with the transfer, transportation and ultimate disposal of a major portion of the solid waste of Karachi city. The common citizen was the most important stakeholder in the success or otherwise of this change. The project implementation was entrusted to KMC and Pakistan Railways, so they had a stake in the project. The project was a part of the then Prime Minister and the politically elected administrator's reform package to the city, so their stakes were also important. In addition, the private contractors, involved in loading, un-loading etc. also had major stakes.

How the change was sustained?

The political scene of the city had changed significantly and the project was officially closed during the caretaker government's rule in Sindh Province in the fall of 1996, when only in the preliminary stages of implementation.

What was the impact of change?

Positive Impacts

- Launching of an initiative which addressed the long term needs of the city by putting forward an integrated planning mechanism.

- Inputs of important segments of civil society like the academic institutions were taken into consideration, though on a less than desired scale.

- Alternative systems of management like privatisation of services were explored.

- Acquisition of substantial land by KMC, which could be put to beneficial use in the future.

- Increase in public awareness of the existence of alternative systems and models of solid waste management.

- For the staff of KMC, the prospect of planning, implementing and managing such a multifaceted project, involving a broad range of public, private and informal individuals, corporation and organisations meant a new experience and a significant change in the existing management and administrative procedures would have required an enhancement in the technical and managerial skills of KMC staff.

Negative impacts

- Although some basic level of information about the project was made available to the general public, the required level of public support was not gathered, with the result that when the project was ultimately abandoned, no real public reaction was witnessed.

- As the project could never be fully implemented, new models of management, for example, privatisation, operation and maintenance of landfill sites etc. and activities such as enhanced staff training and development could not be adequately and effectively tested.

- Growth of a feeling among the KMC staff that the existing system is incapable of effectively responding to the long term needs of the city or tackling new challenges.

End Notes:

[1]   Taka is the currency of Bangladesh.
      In 1999 1 UK £ = 80 Taka approximately.

[2]   There are regular meetings of selected Ward Commissioners and DCC
      officials to discuss issues of solid waste management in the city.

[3]   The old part of Dhaka is perhaps the most congested area in the city,
      with vertical growth and narrow streets.

[4]   Ward Commissioner (in Dhaka) or a councilor (in Pakistan) is an
      elected representative who represent people in a local council.

[5]   The terms, cleaners, sanitary workers and sweepers are used to indicate
      the person who collect waste from streets and houses.

[6]   A demountable container is used to contain waste. It could be loaded
      to special lorries for transportation and un-loading at the disposal site.

[7]   A councilor's ward is the area from where he / she has been elected.

[8]   Rupees is the currency of Pakistan.
      In 1999 1 UK £ = 85 Rupees approximately.

[9]   Faisalabad Area Upgrading Project (FAUP) is a co-funded project by
      the Governments of Pakistan and UK. It aims to improve the quality of
      life of the poor communities residing in the low income areas of Shadab
      Colony, Noorpura, Chak-7and Islamnagar with a total population of
      sixty thousand.

[10] Katchi Abadi is a term used to indicate a low-income settlement with
      very few basic services and infrastructure.

Back cover

Sponsored by DFID etc.

This briefing note presents the findings of a focused research into the 'actual processes of change in low income countries' carried out as a part of the Knowledge and Research Programme (KAR) of the Department for International Development (DFID), UK. The project (R 7143) aims to build capacities of government and non-government organisations in primary collection of solid waste. This briefing note is written for organisations and individuals who in one way or another support the development of solid waste systems in low income countries.

Printed in the USA
CPSIA information can be obtained
at www.ICGtesting.com
JSHW012046140824
68134JS00034B/3286